GOOD MORNING, LORD

Devotions for the Quiet Time

TOMMY CHUPP

BAKER BOOK HOUSE
Grand Rapids, Michigan

First printing, September 1973
Second printing, May 1976

Copyright © 1973
by Baker Book House Company

Printed in the United States of America

TO

Dr. Lee Roberson

Founder and President of
Tennessee Temple Schools
Pastor of
Highland Park Baptist Church
Chattanooga, Tennessee
a Christian gentleman and
a Christian leader
of the highest magnitude

1 ABBREVIATED JOURNEY

"Boast not thyself of tomorrow; for thou knowest not what a day may bring forth."—Proverbs 27:1

Months and months had been spent in final preparation for the journey. The 11½-foot sailboat made of styrofoam had been checked and rechecked. The sails were new and tested. Map and compass rested in the hands of the able seaman, Captain Lang Smith. Today was the big day, long awaited.

Smith cast off from the pier in his seaworthy vessel twenty-five miles south of North Vancouver, British Columbia. His goal was to sail around the world, a trip of fifty thousand miles. The estimated time for the venture was two and a half years.

Nothing could stop Smith now. He was on his way to adventure and new and wonderful experiences. But, alas, the unforseen and unexpected happened. Fifty-five miles out he hit a submerged log near the east end of Vancouver Island and was forced to call off the quest.

Life is much like Smith's "abbreviated journey." Men make great plans and boast of great feats and victories that await them on the horizon of tomorrow—only to find disappointment and heartbreak.

The Scripture for today warns us to be careful not to boast of tomorrow. Rather than boast of tomorrow's victories, let us apply our hands and hearts to the work of today. The question that should be foremost with us is: Will the work I do and the plans I make glorify the Lord Jesus Christ? or self?

We had better make every day count for God. The long life we anticipate may be, in God's plan, an "abbreviated journey."

2 SIN INHERITED

"Wherefore, as by one man sin entered into the world, and death by sin; and so death passed upon all men, for that all have sinned."—Romans 5:12

"Behold, I was shapen in iniquity; and in sin did my mother conceive me."—Psalm 51:5

A leading authority associated with a national mental health institute reports there is growing evidence that all kinds of sick behavior, including alcoholism and criminality, may be inheritable. He further stated there may be more than 60 million schizophrenics in the U.S. population of 200 million. These people have multiproblem behavioral disorders.

King David said the same things the doctor said, but he was more emphatic. David believed in the depravity of man. The Doctor said the outward symptoms of sin, such as alcoholism and criminality, *may* be inheritable. David *knew* they were.

Paul, writing to the Romans, not only acknowledged universal depravity through Adam, but points out the ultimate results of rejecting Jesus Christ. The results are eternal death and separation from Christ our Savior and God the Father. Yes, we are all sinners by nature—by inheritance. There is not one sin man is not capable of committing. Apart from Jesus Christ we are all guilty and there is no escape from the penalty of sin. But there is power for our weakness, grace for our guilt, love for our soul, and forgiveness for our sin through Jesus Christ our Lord and Savior.

3 I DON'T WANT TO DIE

"The gift of God is eternal life through Jesus Christ our Lord."—Romans 6:23

"Boast not thyself of tomorrow for thou knowest not what a day may bring forth."—Proverbs 27:1

"There is no cure," the doctor said. "There is no medication for it." If the man were lucky he would live one year. The doctor's diagnosis and verdict had been given. A one-time newsman was now the object of continuing news, for a man lives and also dies one day at a time.

He had an incurable, a fatal disease, the same disease that killed the great baseball player of bygone years, Lou Gehrig. The dying man related how many nights he dreamed about dying and attending his own funeral; how he feared reading the obituary page each day, and how he wished he could stop the clocks from ticking and make time stand still.

This in itself is a sad story of a man in his fading existence; but there is a heartbreaking climax—he stated he believed in God, but "as to a new life after death on earth, I'll just have to wait and see." Then became evident the sad condition common to those who do not have a firm faith in life after death. The man said, "I don't want to die!"

Just think, one year before death! But also think how much peace of heart the dying man could have had if only he had accepted the free gift of God—eternal life, eternal security.

But remember this: Each of us is dying—a day at a time. Have you accepted as your very own the "gift of God"? Let us not boast of tomorrow, for tomorrow may never come— for you.

4 YOUR WORD

"When thou vowest a vow unto God, defer not to pay it."
Ecclesiastes 5:4

"Your nights and your mornings don't come together." This is a South African expression related to me by Mrs. Bob Moore, the wife of Pastor Moore of the Marietta Baptist Tabernacle in Marietta, Georgia.

The South Africans are very, very sensitive to promises made by their people. They expect a person to do what he promises. That makes sense, doesn't it?

The writer of Ecclesiastes wrote through the leadership of the Holy Spirit that each of us is to be honest before God. What is there to gain in lying to God? So many of our vows are faithless, empty promises! The tragedy therein is that He knows our lying hearts and the content of every empty promise we make.

Do you remember the last promise you made to God? Did you keep it? Have you ever promised to be a better Christian and serve Him more faithfully? Did you keep that promise?

Take inventory for a few minutes and see how well you measure up to the promises you have made to God.

Remember—you gave God "your word"! The South African would ask, "Do your mornings and nights come together?"

5 YOU ARE IMPORTANT

"God is no respecter of persons."—Acts 10:34

Without fear or favor the meter-maid approached the expired meter, looked the car over, pulled out her ticket book, and began to write.

As she wrote the ticket, the car's owner came huffing and puffing at a gallop. "Wait a minute," he yelled. "I just went to get change."

The young lady smiled, tore out the ticket, presented it to the man and said, "I've heard that before." Without fear or favor she handed the ticket to none other than her husband.

She performed her work without prejudice, without consideration of the position or station of the offender. Peter wrote a tremendous truth to each of us concerning God's impartiality in Acts 10:34.

Aren't you glad He loves you regardless of your station in life, your looks, personality, intelligence, ability, and even your lack of service after salvation? Another truth we must accept is that He will one day look into our faces, without respect of personage, and judge our failures. If you think seriously about His love and His judgment of your lack of service, you can't help but want to serve Him.

With God—you are important!

6 YOU'RE BEING WATCHED

"For there is nothing covered, that shall not be revealed; neither hid, that shall not be known."—Luke 12:2

The thieves had planned the robbery over a period of weeks. The night had finally arrived. They approached the radio shop from the rear, gained entrance—and then it happened. They triggered an alarm that switched on floodlights, started five motor-driven cameras, and set off a tape recorder that bellowed over loudspeakers for the police. Their presence and crime were no longer a secret.

The result was one captured thief and an all-out police alert for the other one. His picture had been recorded by the cameras and only time was needed to apprehend him.

Christ told His disciples in Luke 12:2 to always be on guard. Be careful to keep your life clean and spotless for there is "nothing covered," He told them.

Just as surely as the thieves were caught for their crime, so will man face a judging God one day. Those secret sins of life are not hidden from God. He sees, and He knows the heart of man. He remembers our sins, if not confessed, and will hold us accountable for them.

The presence of sin in man's life does not go unseen by God for "there is nothing covered that will not be revealed."

Challenge: Read I John 1:9—*now!*

7 IN THE NICK OF TIME

"Underneath are the everlasting arms."—Deuteronomy 33:27

With wrinkled brow and flushed face, the home builder related what had happened the previous day: He had shown a beautiful home to a new couple in our area. The wife fell in love with the house, and the husband was delighted at the prospect of finding such a good buy.

Everything was going well. The couple and builder had moved to the front yard below the porch. Suddenly the young son came running out of the house and off the edge of the porch which was about twelve feet above the ground.

What could have been a tragedy was avoided because the father was "in the right place in the nick of time." He caught his son as he fell over the edge and saved him from plummeting to the pavement below. (Needless to say, the incident killed the sale.)

How wonderful it is to have the arms of God for our spiritual support. The Scripture says that His arms are "everlasting arms." It should be a source of joy to know that we are secure forever in His arms of love. The fearful child; the ailing, weakened saint; the brokenhearted ones; and every man, woman, boy, and girl needs the security of His tender, divine embrace.

It's refreshing to know He is with us not only "in the nick of time" but *all the time,* for He said, "I will never leave thee, nor forsake thee" (Heb. 13:5).

8 PERMANENT PACEMAKER FOR YOUNGEST INFANT

"For when ye were yet without strength, in due time Christ died for the ungodly."—Romans 5:6

The human body is a fantastic machine. Modern science is likewise amazing. And when science is used in the service of the human body—well, sometimes it's hard to believe the results.

The picture I hold in my hand is of a twenty-six-hour-old infant. The child, shown in an incubator, was born with a heart blockage which prevented her heart from beating more than fifty times a minute. To save her life, she was attached to a temporary pacemaker. Two days later a permanent device was surgically installed in the tiny body.

The tiny infant lived because someone cared for her. She is small, weak, and helpless, but those who love her invested in her future because they valued her life.

The Scripture for today reflects on the weakness and helplessness of man and relates to us the wonderful news: Somebody cared! Somebody loved us in our most sinful condition. The unsaved person has heart trouble worse than that of this tiny child. Aren't you glad God sent the peacemaker—the "Permanent Pacemaker"—the Lord Jesus Christ, for heartsick and sinsick man?

The operation on the infant was costly. So was that which corrects the sinner's heart trouble. But sinful man does not have to pay the price! The blood of Jesus Christ cleanses from all unrighteousness and the Great Physician is waiting for the troubled heart.

Have you accepted Christ? If not, you have heart trouble far more serious than that of the infant. Take time for a "check-up"—*now*. O.K.?

9 MIRROR, MIRROR ON THE WALL

"For I acknowledge my transgressions: and my sin is ever before me."—Psalm 51:3

The old African chief stood proudly on the trail, his body spotted with ashes and with long scars covering his torso. With an attitude of determination he pushed out his chest and said, "Chief is pretty."

The missionary was his friend and he stood his ground just as firmly. He replied, "No, Chief is not pretty."

The injuries that had produced the scars had been inflicted by the chief himself to impress others with his bravery. He also considered them marks of beauty.

Finally the missionary produced a mirror and held it up before the chief. Seeing the ugly form of his own body in the mirror, the chief jerked it from the missionary's hand and smashed it to pieces.

If man would only look into God's perfect mirror, the Bible, and see himself as God sees him. But man would rather hide from the truth and trample God's Word underfoot, just as the old chief would not see himself as others saw him.

In the Scripture for today, David prayed for forgiveness and cried out, "My sin is ever before me." If we will only see ourselves as David saw himself and face the truth, then there can be forgiveness for sin.

Do yourself a favor. Look in the Book, God's precious and perfect mirror. What do you see?

10 FREE STEAK DINNERS

"Whosoever believeth in him should not perish, but have everlasting life."—John 3:16

A man who remains "totally anonymous" provided $3,200 worth of catered steak dinners to inmates at the San Francisco county jails recently.

The twelve hundred inmates received the special Easter meal of sirloin steak, baked potato, salad, vegetables, rolls and cake—and it did not cost them one cent.

What a wonderful Easter gift to prisoners! They did not deserve or expect such a gracious gift, but someone cared enough to give them a meal they will never forget.

How about your Easter gift? If you are unsaved, you are a prisoner of sin and of his satanic majesty, the devil.

Christ saw our spiritual hunger and need, and in tender, loving mercy He came, He suffered, He died, He arose the third day, and ascended unto the Father. The price for your Easter gift has been paid! The Scripture for today tells us "whosoever," and that includes each of us. Only twelve hundred prisoners in the county jails were fed, but Christ died for *all* men.

The steak dinner satisfied the hunger of the men for a few hours, but Christ satisfies forever. Have you accepted His Easter gift? Accept Him today and satisfy the hunger of your soul.

11 THE VALUE OF AN OLD LETTER

Scripture Reading: II John

Recently a letter—of only three pages—was auctioned for $6,000. The letter, written by Mary Lincoln, discussed the possible implication of President Andrew Johnson in her husband's assassination. A book shop in New York bought the letter for the highest price ever recorded for a signed letter of a "First Lady."

I opened my Bible to the Second Epistle of John. Here is one of the most beautiful letters ever written. The writer was the apostle John as led by the Holy Spirit. The letter is short, but the truth and love therein are priceless.

The letter by Mrs. Lincoln is of historical interest but that is all. The letter of John is not only of historical importance but is also a light for the pathway before us.

In II John the Holy Spirit wrote of God's grace, the walk of love and truth, warnings against false teachings and teachers, and the Christian's reward for faithful service.

How much is this short letter worth to you? How often do you read His Word, the Holy Bible?

If you had your choice of the Lincoln letter or God's letter, which would you take?

The value of an old letter—$6,000, or priceless?

12 JACKIE, TAMI AND BARRY

"Present your bodies a living sacrifice. . . . "—Romans 12: 1

Jackie, a fifteen-year-old, is a wonderfully aggressive base-ball player, a terrific rollerskater, and is working on a Red Cross life-saving certificate.

Tami was a bright-eyed nine-year-old. She loved school, was concerned about everybody, and reached for success in everything she attempted.

Barry was a promising young football player in 1959. To-day he sorts silverware in a 706-room hotel where he has been employed since 1967. He plans to enter law school in the near future.

So what's so unusual about these young people, you ask? Jackie has only one leg. Her right leg and hipbone were blown away in a shotgun accident when she was two years old.

Tami had leukemia. She told her teacher one day, "I wish I could have just one day when I didn't feel sick." She was reserved, shy; but she was also loving and thoughtful.

Barry is blind. He was injured in a football game. But his physical blindness has not blinded his outlook on life. He works and lives for each new day's challenges and oppor-tunities.

So you think you have troubles, do you? Each of us should accept the gift of life just as happily and aggressively as Jackie and Barry do, and with the consideration for others that Tami always showed.

Remember what the Word says—"Present your body a living sacrifice." Be glad for the opportunity to live and serve Him who loved us and gave Himself for us.

13 THE IMPORTANCE OF LOVE

"Love one another, as I have loved you."—John 15:12

"A heart attack may depend on how well the person is loved," a very prominent doctor recently reported. "The prevention of disease depends on the psychological as well as the social climate the person lives in," he added.

A study was made of two hundred women who suffered complications after giving birth to their first babies. It was discovered that those who had had to make recent social adjustments—changing residence, quitting a job—with little warm support from family or husband stood a 90 percent chance of complications, while those who felt well-loved ran only a 30 percent chance. The doctor in the study further stated that he thought lack of love was the major factor for the higher incidence of infant deaths and diseases of all kinds among ghetto dwellers.

Is it any wonder that Christ commanded us to love one another? If we are in Christ spiritually through the new birth, then Christ should be seen in us by others in the way we treat or love them. To love the "unlovely" is a difficult task; but if He can love us, bad as we are, then through Christ we *can* and *must* love others.

If loving others is a problem for you, then why not strengthen yourself with the strength of Christ, as the apostle Paul challenges us to do in Philippians 4:13, "I can do all things through Christ which strengtheneth me."

Did you know that someone needs *your* love today?

14 THE FUNERAL ARRANGER

"It is better for me to die than to live."—Jonah 4:8

Three months before his death, Stanley Dorbuck, sixty-three, called a local mortuary to make arrangements for his own funeral. He told the secretary that he did not want to burden anyone with the details, that his money was running out, and that he was about to starve and had no one to help him.

It's a shame when an individual loses faith and hope. Why do men become despondent and weary with life? In the case of Mr. Dorbuck, it was due to advancing age, lack of money, and no friends.

In the case of Jonah in the Scripture, it was because he would not accept the will of God. He became angry with God and tried to convince God that he would be better off dead than alive.

How about you, my friend? How do you face life? Do you face each day's surprise with a positive, vibrant outlook, or with the downhearted countenance of a Dorbuck or Jonah?

When Satan plagues you with disenchantment with life, then check your goal. Can you say as Paul said, "For me to live is Christ"? Or do you turn to the way of Jonah and wish for a speedy end to life?

It's great to be alive!

15 TURNING TRIALS INTO BEAUTY

"As many as I love, I rebuke and chasten."—Revelation 3:19

The oyster is a strange and sensitive creature. It must open its two shells a little to let in seawater from which it takes oxygen and morsels of food. Everything goes well—until a grain of sand or a tiny sea creature settles between the oyster and its shell.

The oyster's soft body is very sensitive to foreign matter, so it paints the inside of its home with a pearly substance, called "nacre," secreted from its body. The intruding foreign body also gets a pearly coat and will continue to get a covering for the rest of the oyster's life. The result is known to us as a pearl. A medium-sized pearl takes at least ten years to be made.

About fifty years ago the oyster fell prey to the impatience of man. A small bead was placed inside the shell and the oyster coated it with nacre. We call these coated beads "cultured pearls." It takes only four years to form them, compared to the ten years for naturally developed pearls.

Man must learn to live with the irritations of life just as the oyster does. God oftimes sends "grains" of chastening into our spiritually sensitive lives. Instead of the frustration and distress we so often show, He really wants the result of our testing to culminate in growth spiritually. Each "grain" He sends should make us more beautiful in His sight, just like the oyster turns its trial into beauty.

Next time He allows a "grain" to enter your life, remember the oyster and turn your trial into beauty.

16 BREAD THAT KEEPS

"I am the bread of life: he that cometh to me shall never hunger."—John 6:35

Bread—the staff of life—has always been known as a good source of both energy and nutrition. Besides the energy it provides, bread is 10 percent protein and is an important source of iron and the B vitamins.

When the Apollo 16 astronauts blasted off to the moon they carried a supply of specially processed bread. The bread was baked and cooled, then passed through a 3,000 degree F. flame to eliminate surface bacteria and mold. After being sliced by a chlorine-washed and flame-sanitized slicing machine, the loaves were heatsealed in sterile bags and subjected to a low dose of irradiation. The last step was to seal each slice individually in transparent, nonflamable plastic film.

What a terrific amount of processing, expense and time! That bread will remain fresh for about a year—and that's good.

But I know of a better bread, one that will last forever. In the Scripture for today, Christ likens Himself to bread. He is the bread that gives life eternal—not just a daily sustenance which is so soon gone. There is never a spiritual void when Christ is allowed to feed the soul.

Yes, Christ is "the bread that keeps." The hungry soul would do well to feed on the Living Bread—Jesus Christ.

17 THE RUNAWAY

"Not forsaking the assembling of ourselves together . . ."
—Hebrews 10:25.

An eleven-year-old girl hid out for twenty-three days and nights in a cramped space underneath a neighbor's house. Her reason? She hated school.

She existed on canned goods taken from neighbors' garages and from her father's camper parked two doors away. When found by her father she was "unkempt" after three weeks without a bath, but she was in good physical condition.

The problem with the girl was that she did not want to accept the responsibility of going to school every day. She left home, father, cleanliness, good food, and responsibility behind. This little girl is to be pitied.

But there are adults who run away from their responsibility and they deserve no pity. The responsibility I speak of is church attendance. When men and women, boys and girls stay away from the church, they are running from the blessings of fellowship, good spiritual food, and peace of heart.

Do you know any "run-aways"?

18 ANGELA'S PROBLEM

"The righteous cry, and the Lord heareth, and delivereth them out of all their troubles."—Psalm 34:17

Three-year-old Angela was brokenhearted. She had lost her most cherished possession, her doll Suzie. It might sound inconsequential to an adult, but to little Angela, it was a problem of mammoth proportions.

Angela told her father, a police detective, exactly what the problem was and described Suzie. A crude drawing of Suzie appeared in the newspaper in Bletchley, England, and in a few hours, Angela had Suzie back in her arms.

There are lessons in this simple story that each of us would do well to learn. Angela had problem. She told her father. She trusted her father. He loved her. He solved her problem. Angela was happy again.

The Scripture for today, says that when we have a problem and cry to our Heavenly Father, He hears us. We, like Angela, should go to our Father with our problems, trust our Father, and expect a solution to our problems. Why? Because He loves us. We are *His* children.

Got a problem? Why not trust our Heavenly Father? The psalmist said, "The righteous cry, and the Lord heareth, and delivereth them out of all their troubles."

I like the word *all* in the verse, don't you?

19 TOO HOT TO HANDLE

"Touch not the unclean thing."—II Corinthians 6:17

Pastor Bob Moore tells the story about the man who walked into the blacksmith's shop and reached into the water tank to get a horseshoe from the bottom. No sooner had he brought it to the surface than he dropped it. "What's the matter," inquired the blacksmith, "was it hot?" The man stood there shaking his hand. "No sir!" he said, "It just doesn't take me long to look at horseshoes."

You're right, friend. It didn't take him long to find out he could get burned. It was too hot to handle! An intelligent appraisal of the possible outcome would have prevented the burn, wouldn't it?

In the Scripture for today, God has instructed us concerning our separation from sin and all appearances of sin. Yet we rush into situations instead of seeking His will. Invariably we grab hold of sin, find it too hot to handle, and end up like the man in Brother Moore's story. We get burned and so many times we carry the scars of sin's burn for the rest of our lives. Our testimony too, and an effective life for Christ loses its value because of sin's burn.

If we would only remember—sin is "too hot to handle."

20 AMBITIONS

"He that winneth souls is wise."—Proverbs 11:30

A man in London, an amateur violinist, spent 1,200 pounds ($3,120) to fulfill his lifelong ambition. He had always wanted to conduct his own orchestra, so he hired the entire Royal Philharmonic Orchestra.

He commented, "Some people think I'm mad, but my wife recently inherited some money and she insisted I blow it all on this one concert."

Ambition certainly pushes some folks to strange deeds, doesn't it? A young lady in New York recently demonstrated a talent she says is "something I was born with." Using three standard pieces of bubble gum, the college freshman masterfully (?) blew a gigantic bubble nine inches in diameter. She immediately claimed it a record, had the bubble notarized, and stated she would send the information to the *Guinness Book of World Records*.

Ambitions are good, because they spur us on toward accomplishing goals. Personally, I find it hard to appreciate the two realized ambitions related above. On the contrary, I do not find it hard to appreciate the ambition we are challenged to accept from the Scripture chosen for today.

Music, bubbles, or souls—which will last throughout eternity as a result of your ambitions? Get the message? ". . . He that winneth souls is wise."

21 STOP SIGNS

"For all have sinned, and come short of the glory of God."
—Romans 3:23

"The wages of sin is death."—Romans 6:23

"Pull over to the curb, son! Didn't you see that stop sign back there?"

The Seattle officer wrote out a ticket to—a pedal-pushing twelve-year-old bike rider! Now that really takes the cake, doesn't it? The nerve of that officer giving a twelve-year-old a $10.00 ticket. What does he have against kids?

Anger against the officer might be your first reaction. But there was a reason for his action. The sergeant at the police department says, "The officer cares a great deal about the children in his area. The purpose of a stop sign is to save lives. A twelve-year-old kid can get killed just as dead on a bike as a forty-year-old man in a car."

Mr. Officer, I apologize. You are exactly right! That ounce of prevention is worth more than many pounds of cure. In fact, there is no comparison, because you can't cure or reclaim life after death.

Our Scripture for today admonishes us to be concerned for those who are running God's "stop signs." We should attempt to stop those speeding through life unaware or disregarding the tragedy ahead—death and eternal separation from God. Sure, we might be misunderstood and spoken against, as the officer was. But we must reach the twelve-year-olds, and the forty- and sixty-year-olds, before life slips away.

Go, stop somebody today as they speed through life. Remember—"all have sinned" and "the wages of sin is death."

22 STOP, THIEF!

"And these things write we unto you, that your joy may be full."—I John 1:4

The U.S. Postal Service reports that although they were able to cut theft losses by 58 percent—from $2,250,000 in 1970 to $934,971 in 1971—stealing from the mails continues to be a serious problem. Postal authorities credited tighter security, a stepped-up assault on burglary gangs, and changes in manpower policies for the major reduction in losses.

Think of that, $934,971 in losses during 1971! This in America, the land of the free and the home of the brave, where churches are plentiful, where law enforcement agencies are plentiful. That's right, in America, your home and mine.

These thefts in many cases must be paid by the government, and that's you and me. This could bother you if you let it; but let me tell you how big a mail thief each of us is, O.K.? God sent us letters in the New Testament for our encouragement, comfort, and instruction. These were sent so that our "joy may be full."

But is our joy full? No, for the most part we lead empty, dull, joyless lives due to our own mail thefts. You see, we rob ourselves because we never read the letters. Everyday we need to go to God's mailbox, the Bible, for His letter of the day to us. This is the only way we can prevent spiritual theft.

By the way, have you been to His mailbox this morning?

23 PEOPLE, PEACE, AND PAUL

"Live in peace. . . ."—II Corinthians 13:11
". . . peace through the blood. . . ."—Colossians 1:20

Swedish inventor Alfred Nobel said, "I wish I could produce a substance or invent a machine of such frightful efficacy for wholesale destruction that wars should thereby become altogether impossible." Mr. Nobel, whose yearly awards go to those making the greatest contributions to building a peaceful world, wanted to make war so terrible, so horrible, that man would never want to bear arms. Yet, the fortune he acquired was the result of his invention of dynamite, which has been a contributing factor to war and unrest. Mr. Nobel hoped for peace, but generation after generation has experienced only discontent, unrest, and war.

I like what Paul wrote in II Corinthians 13:11: "Live in peace." But it seems it is impossible to fulfill God's direction for a peaceful life. These carnal bodies are continually at war with self, others, and the will of God.

Paul was writing to the Christians at Corinth concerning their Christian self-discipline, but the same problems are prevalent today, aren't they? So I'm surely glad Paul spelled out the way to peace: all things can be reconciled through the blood of Christ.

People, peace, and Paul. People haven't changed; peace is still possible in the heart of man; and Paul's message is as relevant today as in the day God gave it to him.

Friend, there is only one way to peace of heart—peace with yourself, God, and people, and that is "through the blood."

24 PRICE TAG

"And be sure your sin will find you out."

—Numbers 32:23

An unusual thing happened in Wurzburg, Germany, recently. It was a beautiful day and shoppers jammed the shops.

The police were suddenly called to an optometrist's shop because of a suspected burglary. They looked over the customers and apprehended a young, bespectacled man as he walked away from the store.

Although the man vehemently denied knowledge of the crime, he was taken into custody. He continued to deny the charge—even though the glasses he was wearing still bore the label and price tag from the burglarized shop.

How ridiculous can a man be? we ask ourselves. He had fooled no one and yet he thought all were fooled.

What about you, my friend? Are you a guilty sinner running from God? If you are, then you should awaken to the fact that you are seen with the price tag of sin openly displayed before God.

The police caught the guilty man. God *always* gets His man. He saves men through the blood of Jesus Christ, or He will one day judge and cast into hell the rejectors of His Son.

Remember, the "price tag" for your sin is ever before Him.

25 I'LL NEVER FORGET

"And in hell he lift up his eyes, being in torments. . . ."—
Luke 16:23

"I'll never forget," a congressman recently exclaimed as
he emerged from a prison. He had voluntarily lived the life
of an inmate for thirty-six hours.

He was stripped, fingerprinted, and given a number, No.
1104. Next he was thrown into "the hole," and harassed by
guards. The unshaven congressman said he had no privacy,
no freedom of movement, no paper, no pencils, no books. He
stated, "It's hard to describe what it does to you. The emo-
tional strain is tremendous."

He went through the ordeal in order to gain a better un-
derstanding of prison life.

I believe God gave us the account of the rich man in hell
in order that we who read of his agony and distress would
never forget.

Do you believe the Bible is God's Word? Do you believe it
is profitable to you as a guide as well as a warning? Do you
believe hell is as terrible as the rich man said it was?

If you believe the account in Luke 17, then I hope you can
say as the congressman said, "I'll never forget."

26 THE EMPTY TANK

"Speak every man truth with his neighbour."—Ephesians 4:25

A thirty-six-year-old mystery in North Bay, New York, has finally been cleared up.

Three dozen years ago the gas was stolen from a power shovel in the gravel pits. After years of living with guilt, the thief sent a note to a local official in North Bay. The note read as follows:

"To whom it may concern: In 1936 I stole some gas from the power shovel in the gravel pit. Enclosed find check for $5.00 to pay for same."

Guilt is the shadow that chases and hovers over the conscience of man till he sets his life aright, confesses, faces the penalty, and pays the price for his wrongdoing.

How is your conscience today? Are there some problems of guilt in your life because of theft, or of unkindness or mistreatment to someone somewhere at sometime in the past?

It's so wonderful to get things right with others, for then you get things right with God.

"Speak every man truth with his neighbour."

27 THE TRUTH ABOUT LYING

"A false witness shall not be unpunished, and he that speaketh lies shall not escape."—Proverbs 19:5

A poll was taken at a large college recently and students were found to be honest about one thing in particular—*lying*.

There were three major causes given for lying. First was the fear of punishment—31.3 percent. Second—at 24.3 percent—was the wish to avoid hurting someone. The third reason—at 18.3 percent—was the desire to avoid a disagreeable situation.

The students were also asked under what circumstance a lie would be acceptable and 32.9 percent said, "To avoid hurting someone." Another 22.6 percent said, "To protect someone."

The lie that hurts someone else was registered as the "most unforgivable" and rated a negative 54.3 percent vote.

The big question is: Is it ever justifiable to lie? What is your answer? If your vote is in tune *with* the students polled, then you are *out* of tune with the Word of God.

The writer of Proverbs states that "he that speaketh lies shall not escape." What God expects is clean, honest hearts that love and speak the truth.

Is God getting what He expects from you?

28 BREATHING

"He giveth to all life, and breath, and all things."—Acts
17:25

Inhale, exhale, inhale, exhale, inhale, exhale—did you
ever realize how wonderful breathing is? Unconsciously, an
adult takes around sixteen breaths a minute which adds up
to a grand total in twenty-four hours of around nineteen
thousand inhales and exhales.

We breath faster when exercising, and slowest—six to
eight breaths a minute—when we sleep. Adult lungs hold
about four quarts of air. With each breath approximately a
pint of stale air is exhaled and a pint of fresh air inhaled.

The Master Engineer, God Almighty, made a remarkable
machine when He made man. Paul relates to us in the Scripture how wonderful God is to us, for He is the giver of "life,
and breath, and all things."

Isn't that tremendous? Life, breath—and all things. The
"all things" are in relation to the blessings of life He gives to
us and which so often we take so lightly.

Take time today to reflect on His goodness to us. Why is
He so good to us? The answer is simple—yet so profound—
He loves us!

29 THE LAST WISH

"The wicked is driven away in his wickedness; but the righteous hath hope in his death."—Proverbs 14:32

"Not near the clubhouse, he didn't like the clubhouse. He said he came out to see the horses, not the people."

Finally the young man and his sister picked a flower bed in front of the grandstand to be their father's final resting place. This man, who had loved horses and had gambled away three fortunes at the races, had left instructions to have his body cremated and the ashes scattered at Hialeah Race Track, for, "Hialeah was my father's idea of heaven," his son said.

Tonight my Bible fell open at the signature of Dr. Charles F. Weigle and his favorite verse, Philippians 1:21, "For me to live is Christ, and to die is gain." What a blessing it was to have known the beloved writer of "No One Ever Cared for Me Like Jesus."

Do you know what his dying wish was as he, at ninety-four, lay on the hospital bed? He said, "I want to go home." The nurses were concerned about this until Dr. Lee Roberson, Dr. Weigle's pastor, explained that he wanted to go "home" to heaven.

The ashes of Hialeah will be remembered by only a few, but Dr. Weigle lives on through his music. His love for Christ and his work as a soldier of the King inspires all who knew him.

The author of Proverbs wrote, "The righteous hath hope in his death." That's the way it is.

By the way, what is your last wish?

30 CHICKEN PLUCKERS

"Whatsoever thy hand findeth to do, do it with thy might; for there is no work, nor device, nor knowledge, nor wisdom, in the grave, whither thou goest."—Ecclesiastes 9:10

The ladies in the picture I just cut out of the paper are four of the happiest ladies I have seen in a long time. These ladies compose a world championship team that really makes the feathers fly!

You may have guessed it by now. These ladies make up the world's champion chicken plucking team. They plucked three chickens each in a fraction over four minutes in Spring Hill, Florida, beating the time of all other would-be "chicken plucker" champions.

I think there is an area of dedication here that must be reckoned with. They accepted a challenge and would not take second best.

Every Christian would do well to put himself into the work of the Lord as completely as these ladies applied themselves to theirs. The verse for today says, "Whatsoever thy hand findeth to do, do it with thy might." Then it reminds us that there is no work for us in the grave. If we are ever going to do anything for God don't you think we ought to start *today?*

Remember the "chicken pluckers."

31 SLEEPING LIKE A LOG

"Love not sleep, lest thou come to poverty."—Proverbs
20:13

I have heard the statement "sleeping like a log" since I
was a child. Not until recently was I assured a person could
sleep so soundly, however. I refer to an article I clipped from
the February 7, 1972, issue of the local newspaper.

A sixty-one-year-old gentleman from Burns, Oregon, suffered the misfortune of having his car stall just as he began
to cross the railroad tracks. He couldn't get the car to start;
so, because a cold wave had set in that morning and he was
very sleepy, he wrapped himself in a blanket and went to
sleep in the car.

You guessed it! While he was snoozing, a freight train hit
the car. Although extensive damage was caused to the car,
the geriatric sleepyhead was found unharmed, wrapped in his
blanket and still asleep when the authorities arrived.

The writer of Proverbs admonishes us to be alert, awake.
He tells us not to love or covet sleep. We are to be busy and
active, living the life God has given us.

Are you asleep on the highway of life?

32 THE CHILD KILLER

"From a child thou hast known the holy scriptures, which are able to make thee wise unto salvation through faith which is in Christ Jesus."—II Timothy 3:15

The mother held her two small daughters by the hand as the train pulled into the Harlem station. It was a beautiful Sunday afternoon and the children, aged three and five, held on tightly in the shuffle of people amid the noise of the approaching train.

Suddenly tragedy struck. The mother, holding fast to both daughters, plunged directly into the path of the onrushing engine. The mother and the five-year-old were killed. The three-year-old was seriously injured.

The police called it suicide, murder, and attempted murder. The mother had deliberately pulled both children off the platform, intending that all three should die.

I have met another kind of "child killer" lately. This kind clutches the hands of their children so tightly that they are shielded from the Gospel of Jesus Christ. You ask, "But is that 'child killing'?" Yes! Here we have a threat of death worse than the approaching train, for children kept from Christ suffer eternal death and spiritual separation from God forever.

What a great testimony Timothy could give. The Word says he heard the Scriptures from his earliest childhood. Who took the time to teach him? In II Timothy 1:5 we see the beautiful example of faith, love, and leadership he received from his grandmother Lois and his mother Eunice. They cared enough to share with Timothy the Lord Jesus Christ and therefore he was "made wise unto salvation" (II Tim. 3:15).

Do you know any "child killers"?

33   HERE PIGGIE, PIGGIE, HERE

"Giving thanks always for all things unto God and the Father in the name of our Lord Jesus Christ."—Ephesians 5:20

The story is told of a kindly old man from the country who went into a city restaurant for lunch. The Christian farmer found a table near a group of young men, ordered his food, then quietly bowed his head and offered thanks for the food.

The young men thought they would embarrass the old man with ridicule so one of them asked him loudly, "Hey, old man, does everyone do that where you come from?"

The old man looked at the young man and said quietly, "No, son, the hogs don't."

Did you ever see the hogs fed or, as we said in the country, "slopped"? It's a simple matter. All you do is dump all the scraps over the fence into the trough, then stand back! You never *heard* such enjoyable eating in all your life. Then, after the meal is over, do the hogs smile, wipe their lips, and say "thank you?" You're right, the eating *is* loud but the courtesy and etiquette are not to be found.

But wait a minute! I know some Christians as well as un-saved people who take all the blessings of God, enjoy them to their full, yet never utter a "thank you" heavenward. How about you? Is there a continual "thank you" given to God for "all things" as the Scripture commands us do, or is your life a pig pen of ingratitude?

Here piggie, piggie, here!

34 SQUEALING, SHINY SHOES

"For God shall bring every work into judgment, with every secret thing, whether it be good, or whether it be evil."
—Ecclesiastes 12:14

I read an interesting article from Kalamazoo, dated March 3, 1971, concerning a pair of shiny shoes. The article related that a man is serving a three- to four-year jail sentence because a pair of shoes "squealed" on him. The man, twenty-one years old, was charged with putting on a new pair of shoes at a shopping center and walking out without paying for them.

He would never have been caught, he said, had not the shoes "squealed" on him.

Wait a minute! I read of a more astonishing incident than the above. In Portland, Oregon, while a trial went on in the courtroom of a very prominent circuit judge, a thief lifted a wallet with $12.00 from the court bailiff, and a coin purse with $3.00 from the court reporter.

How about that! In open daylight the court bailiff and court reporter were relieved of their money.

The Scripture for today says that all works will be judged by God, every secret thing; nothing goes unseen by Him who ever watches. Are we ever guilty of stealing? How about the *time* God has given us to serve, *bodies* to be yielded to Him, *talents* to use at His bidding?

Who is really the worse thief—the shoe thief, the court thief, or you and me?

35 4:00 A.M. AND WIDE AWAKE

"Seest thou a man diligent in his business? he shall stand before kings."—Proverbs 22:29

I hold in my hand the obituary of a man who lived to the age of eighty. He arose at 4:00 A.M. and dictated an average of twenty thousand words a day. His books are read by kings and rulers as well as by the everyday man. The man was Erle Stanley Gardner, the creator of the Perry Mason mysteries. What was so unusual about Mr. Gardner? He loved to work.

Another man who loved to work was J. C. Penney, the founder of the national chain of department stores that bear his name. He died at the age of ninety-six.

Both of these men rose early, worked hard, put in long hours, enjoyed their work—and enjoyed success and a long life. They were what the writer of Proverbs says: "diligent in . . . business." A lesson can be learned from these men—to be a success a person must desire success and work expecting success. Someone put it well when he said, "There is never a time to just sit back and relax."

If this is true, then we have a new way to spell the word *success:* W-O-R-K. That's right, there is really no shortcut to success, whether material or spiritual. God expects us to work to reach others for Him. Being diligent in business gives a right testimony before the world.

Know what time it is? It is time to go to *work*. Good day!

36 CARROTEX XXL

"Run with patience the race that is set before us."—Hebrews 12:1

A great cheer went up when Toy Token Tom, an eight-inch worm, wriggled across the finish line first. This event was billed as the world's first worm race. Included were other "big names": Creepy Crawler, Iggles Squiggles, and Yesman, all of which were far back in the field.

Whippy Willy I was the favorite until he was accidentally squashed during training. His successor, Whippy Willy II came in second by a worm's length.

The winner's home was the area behind the bear pit at Chessington Zoo in Brighton, England. There he enjoyed a simple homelife, you might say. The only unusual thing about Toy Token Tom was the special secret diet his trainer supplied—Carrotex XXL.

Don't you imagine it took a lot of patience on the part of the thirty onlookers who waited, watched—waited, watched . . . and cheered for their favorite?

In the Scripture for today we are admonished to run with patience the race before us. It's a Christian race designed for spiritual progress, and everyone can be a winner *if* he is faithful in "looking unto Jesus the author and finisher of our faith" (Heb. 12:2).

Toy Token Tom had Carrotex XXL for strength and endurance. What is the source of strength for the Christian? The Bible, prayer, and the Holy Spirit.

Have you been getting your nourishment lately?

37   SHE WON—THEN LOST

"And I give unto them eternal life; and they shall never perish, neither shall any man pluck them out of my hand."
—John 10:28

February 21, 1971, marked the fiftieth anniversary of the passing of a remarkable woman—one who died broken-hearted at the age of eighty-six. Mary Walker was a physician, having graduated from Syracuse Medical College in 1855.

During the Civil War she enlisted, thus becoming the only female army surgeon serving the Union Army. Her coolness under fire at Gettysburg and other battles enabled her to save literally hundreds of the wounded.

She was captured and imprisoned by the Confederate forces, but in 1865 she received America's highest military medal, the Congressional Medal of Honor. She is the only woman ever to receive this honor.

An unusual event occurred in 1917. The War Department ruled that the medal should go only to service personnel with properly documented valor in some specific battle. This decision resulted in nine hundred names being removed from the roll of those thus honored. Among them were those of Buffalo Bill Cody and Mary Walker. She lost the honor because "the occasion for its giving was not recorded in War Department Archives." She had won the medal, had worn it for half a century—and then she lost it!

Think a minute about the Scripture for today, John 10:28. *He* said it, *He* meant it, *He* will not take it back. Christ's promises are not retractable and they do not depend on our merit. Once we have been awarded eternal life, it is our possession forever.

38 MIAMI TO CANADA

"Take up his cross, and follow me."—Matthew 16:24

Did you see the picture of the young man trudging down Biscayne Boulevard in Miami shouldering a rugged seven-foot cross en route to Canada? The top of the cross rests on his shoulders and the bottom follows on a pair of wheels much like the training wheels of a child's bicycle. From the cross dangles a sleeping bag with a Bible inside, a pack of potato chips, and a towel for his sweating brow.

He related that two weeks prior to that time he woke up saying, "Yes, Lord, yes, Lord." He further stated, "I knew then I had to lug the cross to gather Christians around the common gospel."

When I read the story and saw the picture I thought of the words of Matthew 16:24. The words of Jesus relate to the suffering of the saved for Christ's sake, persecutions for righteousness' sake, and any affliction that befalls us for His glory. The test for the redeemed in relation to crossbearing is, can we rejoice in afflictions? even glory in them? Then, and only then can we truly say we have taken up *our* cross.

He doesn't expect us to carry our cross from Miami to Canada; no, he expects us to carry it further than that—from salvation till we meet Him in death or in the air.

Oh, yes, I forgot to mention that the last part of the verse reads, "and follow me." It's not a lonely road for He walked it before us, and now He walks with us.

39 MOVING DAY

"Jesus saith unto him, I am the way, the truth, and the life. . . ."—John 14:6

Pack this, store that, put this in the trash, be careful not to break this—sound familiar? Those little phrases are not at all pleasant to my ears! I detest the thought of moving. Not the thought of going to a new home, but the decision after decision of what to keep and what not to keep really gets to me. Isn't it amazing how poor you are until you start packing?

Recently I read of a young couple in Atlanta who decided to "purchase their freedom." The husband said, "I was always taught to work hard and accumulate money, to drink two martinis at lunch and worry about whether or not the client likes me. That's how you get ahead. But it's funny, you find out getting ahead doesn't make you happy."

The couple decided to have a moving day—to a new life. They are planning to build a fifty-foot seagoing ketch and go wherever they desire and stay as long as they wish.

Well, I'll have to hand it to them; they are trying to find happiness. But a change of residence will not supply the needs of man's heart and soul. He may "purchase his freedom," as the young couple says, from four walls and the daily grind. He may think this will bring lasting peace, but it will never suffice.

There is only one way to lasting joy and happiness. The way is Jesus. He said, "I am the way, the truth, and the life." The couple may be excited about "the advantages of leaving this life behind," but Christ is the only real advantage this life has to offer. And He is the only one who can give the everlasting advantages even after "leaving this life behind."

On your "moving day" where will you be taking up your new residence? Heaven or hell?

40 PREVENTING THE THEFT

"Be sober, be vigilant; because your adversary the devil, as a roaring lion, walketh about, seeking whom he may devour."—I Peter 5:8

An unusual story from London relates how the British archaeologists are dealing with treasure hunters. The treasure hunters are using metal detectors to ferret out treasure. The archaeologists, fearing that much local history will be destroyed, are "striking back" by spreading tacks and nails around Hadleigh Castle, Essex, and in Portsmouth to "jam" the metal detectors. They report their efforts have had a "very great effect."

A simple solution to preventing theft, don't you agree? A thief is a rascal to be guarded against as well as caught after the crime.

Aren't you glad God gives us just what we need to protect our treasures in Christ as well as to expose the old thief, Satan? Through Bible study, prayer, claiming His promises, and daily obedience we have all we need to prevent the theft of our greatest spiritual treasure—the peace of knowing we are saved by Christ's sacrifice. And we're one up on the archaeologists—we know who the thief is!

Have you been using these simple means to prevent theft?

41 PERSISTENT ELEANOR

"Let us run with patience the race that is set before us."
—Hebrews 12:1

It has been a long haul for Eleanor McRae. After sixteen years in San Francisco's schools for adults she received her high school diploma at the age of seventy. And she doesn't plan to quit. Immediately after graduating she enrolled in music and sewing courses.

Persistent Eleanor really puts to shame many who start but never finish the task before them. Eleanor mixed that magic ingredient, desire, with a lot of hard work. With such a combination, she could not fail. She reached her goal, and our hats are off to her.

What about your Christian goals, my friend? Paul said he ran with patience, and so must we. Patience in prayer, patience in soul winning, patience in Bible study—patience, patience, patience.

Patient persistence, that's the lesson we can learn from Eleanor as well as from Paul. Today let us be a persistent Eleanor and a patient Paul. O.K.?

42 EAVESDROPPING

"If we say that we have no sin, we deceive ourselves, and the truth is not in us."—I John 1:8

In the not-too-distant future you may be able to make department store and banking transactions via your television set. And your water and electric meters may soon be read in the same way. This is possible because of T.V.'s capacity to radiate energy even while turned off. The device which would make this possible is being tested by cable T.V. specialists in some communities at the present time and is likely to come into limited use in five years.

As is so often the case, a system that has decided advantages carries with it potential disadvantages. Unscrupulous persons could use these scientific discoveries to prey on the public by picking up conversations in homes and offices and relaying them to wiretappers. It's becoming increasingly difficult to maintain a little privacy, isn't it!

Man is such a foolish creature. He thinks that his "secret sins" are known only to himself. In the vernacular, "It just ain't so!"

John wrote that "we deceive ourselves," if we say we have not sinned. There are unseen "eavesdroppers" all about us—the angels of God are watching and listening; the devil and his satanic helpers are ever alert; God is ever present. In I Peter 3:12 the Word says, ". . . the eyes of the Lord are over the righteous, and his ears are open unto their prayers; but the face of the Lord is against them that do evil."

Secret sins? They may be secret from man, but they are not secret to the unseen "eavesdroppers." Careful, my friend, someone is listening!

43 TOO PROUD TO ASK

"Pride goeth before destruction."—Proverbs 16:18

For two and a half days, before their car bogged down in an orange grove, two sisters, one eighty, the other eighty-four years old, drove in circles, confused. The police in rural Lake County found the younger sister just eight miles from the home she was trying to reach. She had died from exposure and exhaustion. The other sister was found in critical condition lying in the shade of an orange tree, her sweater draped over her face to ward off mosquitoes.

A police dispatcher said, "It looks like they were too proud to stop and ask somebody to take them home. They just kept driving, asking directions, and driving. The more they drove, the more confused they became." They drove more than two hundred miles trying to reach their home only twenty miles away. Apparently they drove almost continuously, not even stopping to eat.

What a shame, you say. But I know a more pathetic story about folks "too proud to ask." Only they travel for years instead of days. Years in which pride and self-sufficiency keep them from asking God to help them, with the inevitable consequence of not reaching home, the haven of rest, heaven. "Pride goeth before destruction." The alternative to destruction is found in Romans 10:13: "For whosoever shall call upon the name of the Lord shall be saved."

The sisters were too proud to ask for help. Are you too proud to ask help from Him who forgives and leads the way home?

44 SLEEP, WONDERFUL SLEEP

"How long wilt thou sleep, O sluggard? When wilt thou rise out of thy sleep?"—Proverbs 6:9

Dr. Mangalore Pai believes normal people can thrive on only five to six hours of sleep a night and that the children of A.D. 2000 will be able to get by with as little as three hours. The doctor is ninety years old, retired, and sleeps only three hours a night. His convictions about men being able to elude the "sandman" stem from his experience in the Second World War. Hundreds of hospital beds were set aside, when the war broke out, in order to take care of the avalanche of nervous breakdowns caused by no sleep or broken sleep night after night. Instead of nervous breakdowns, however, the mental health of the people actually improved.

Dr. Pai believes that as man discovers more reasons for staying awake he will need less and less sleep.

The writer of Proverbs also had some ideas about how much time a man should spend sleeping. And don't you believe the Lord Jesus Christ expects an answer from each of us as to how we use the time God gives us? He tells us to pray. We grow weary, lethargic, and pass into dreamland. He says, "Study the Word; Witness for the Lord; Go on visitation." The sluggard, the lazy man, says, "But, Lord, I have to get my rest."

So man sleeps his life away, too lazy to follow the paths God commands him to follow.

I believe Dr. Pai is right when he says, "As man discovers more reasons for staying awake he needs less and less sleep."

What reasons do you have for staying awake?

45 THE RUNAWAYS

"Christ hath redeemed us. . . ."—Galatians 3:13

"Thirty dollars!" the eleven-year-old boy gasped. That's too much! You should start at $25.00 each." The judge had asked bidding to start on each of the three ponies at $30.00.

A conference was quickly called by the judge and the shelter director. They learned that the ponies had run away from the farm, and, after learning their whereabouts, the boy had brought his entire savings of $75.00 to the public auction to reclaim his property. Originally he had purchased the ponies with money he had earned scrubbing floors. Needless to say, there were no opposing bidders and he paid for and took home his runaways.

Did you know that man also is a runaway? That's right; we are runaways by nature and by inheritance. For although God made man loving, honest, and God-fearing, man, tempted by Satan, broke through the fences of obedience God had set up, and he ran away from God (Genesis 3).

But "Christ hath redeemed us"—bought us back and paid the price for the runaway through His sacrifice on the cross. And just as the judge accepted the payment for the ponies, so God accepted the payment Christ made by His death on Calvary as sufficient for every sinner.

What a blessing to realize that the price is paid and that the "runaway" need not run any longer.

The big question is: Are you still a "runaway"?

46 THE BY-PRODUCTS OF TRASH

"All our righteousnesses are as filthy rags."—Isaiah 64:6

From LaVerne, California, comes the story of a plant that turns garbage and trash into oil, metals, glass, and charcoal. The Occidental Petroleum Corporation demonstrated a four-story-high pilot plant that can process four tons of waste a day. A research engineer vacuumed some trash into a pipe, and oil gushed out the other end. The management stated that the by-products of trash can be sold and the money used to pay for some of the cost of collecting America's millions of tons of waste.

Great day in the morning! Just think, the day may come when, instead of paying for garbage pick-up, we are paid for our garbage.

As I read this story I thought of the "garbage" in man's life, moral and spiritual garbage. Isaiah wrote that "all our righteousnesses are as filthy rags." David gave this sad commentary: "There is none that doeth good, no, not one." All of us are as filthy rags, or garbage, in the sight of God until . . . until we are born again, made from waste to worth, from trash to treasure, from filthy sinners to forgiven saints. This is the reason Christ gave His life at Calvary—that He might reclaim, through His blood, men and women, boys and girls.

Wouldn't you say that saved souls are a tremendous by-product from the trash of human degradation?

"Treasure" or "trash," the choice is yours.

47 HOW TO GET OUT OF DEBT

"In whom we have redemption. . . ."—Colossians 1:14

There are more families in debt today than ever before in the history of our nation. While it is easy to get "buried under" debt, it takes skill, deep-down resolution, and hard-headed determination to dig out of the problem.

An economist gives the following suggestions to put one on the road to solvency.

1. Make a chart listing all your debts.
2. Match your income against your fixed expenses. In short, make a budget.
3. Decide where you can cut expenses, then cut.
4. Sell items you no longer need or use.
5. Can you do without that second car? Sell it!
6. Can you moonlight at a second job? (This one is not for "Mr. Lazybones.")

Financial recovery is not impossible if one gives his best; but no matter how man tries he cannot redeem himself spiritually.

Christ, our precious sin-bearer, has paid the price for our sin debt. The cost was too great for us, but not for Him who loved us and gave Himself to redeem us from the curse of the law.

Friend, do you know how to get out of spiritual debt? Paul gives the answer, "In whom we have redemption through his blood, even the forgiveness of sins."

The debt is paid. Now it's up to you whether or not you *accept* His payment for your debt.

48 LIFE-SAVERS

"For God sent not his Son into the world to condemn the world; but that the world through him might be saved."—John 3:17

Two Chattanooga-area citizens were honored by the Chattanooga-area safety council for saving the life of a man trapped in his burning car after it rolled over an embankment on the expressway.

Two men gave their time and risked their lives while others sped by rather than invest their time and effort.

Two looked over the portals of heaven one day and saw man's spiritually wicked life which would eventually end in eternal death in the flames of hell. God the Father and Jesus Christ cared enough to reach out and rescue man, though it cost the life of the Son.

The sad state of affairs is that today men would rather stay stranded along the highways of life, wrecked and trapped, than yield to the life-saver Jesus Christ. Maybe they just haven't heard there is One who cares and rescues. Someone must tell the story. Will you?

49 THE GREAT ESCAPE

"For though I be free from all men, yet have I made my-self servant unto all, that I might gain the more."—I Corinthians 9:19

From Suva, Fiji, the news has come that three men in a boat sailed 450 miles south of Suva to proclaim a wreck-strewn reef a republic. The land, all four hundred acres, is to be reserved "for people who wish to escape crime, riots, drugs, and the present world."

The only realistic appraisal of the plan described above is that man is attempting to escape from responsibility to a haven of comfort and protection. Paul said he was a servant to all men; so is every Christian, for we have a duty before God to shine for Christ and not hide from this present world.

Paul states it very clearly in Romans 14:7 where he writes, "For none of us liveth to himself, and no man dieth to himself."

The Great Escape? What are you hiding from? Salvation? Sin? Service? Dear friend, there is no great escape from Him who is ever watching.

50 STAY CLEAN

"Be sure your sin will find you out."—Numbers 32:23

A good inspector and a bad problem. That was the picture at a university recently written about in a local city paper. Sixty students and seven dormitories came under inspection by the president of the colossal university after he received word that some eighty-five hundred students were bothered with lice.

Through the use of soap and shampoo and special disinfectants, he said, "the situation is under control."

You say, "ugh"; but check your own life and be sure you are not plagued with the parasitic infestation of sin before you pass judgment. The students knew how to stay clean and guard themselves from infestation by the lice, but even more so do we who know Christ know how to stay clean spiritually.

Watch out! The inspector is watching. Stay clean!

51 LOOK OUT!

"Wine is a mocker, strong drink is raging; and whosoever is deceived thereby is not wise."—Proverbs 20:1

I knew a man who said he was saved, yet could not prove himself strong enough to turn from drink. He lost a top management position, and stepped down to managing a single department in a large variety store. He persisted in drink till, out of control of self and vehicle one afternoon, he hit a man, then sped on his way. He tried to cover up his crime, but was traced and apprehended. He lost face, prominence, money, respect, and—if he was saved—he lost his testimony.

Here again we see the old story of "I can handle my liquor"; yet it takes more to meet the attack of Satan than self. One must have Christ, His Word, and prayer.

Look out! You may be next, my friend. Don't be deceived.

52 YOU CAN TAKE IT WITH YOU

*"Your gold and silver is cankered; and the rust of them
shall be a witness against you."*—James 5:3

In an Egyptian museum priceless treasures of gold and
jewels have been discovered hidden under the wrappings of
royal mummies or in the body cavities. These finds were
brought to light by the amazing eye of the X-ray machine.

This recent insight into the ritualistic beliefs of the ancient
Egyptians indicates that men have not changed. Heaping up
riches for self is as much an obsession today as it was in the
Egypt of yesterday. Yet we are warned: Beware, for man's
love of riches will one day turn witness against him. God sees
better than any X-ray machine, and His records are more
complete than any kept by radiologists.

Yet there is a treasure you can take with you. And the
choice is yours to make.

53 WHAT A CONTEST!

"Joy shall be in heaven over one sinner that repenteth."
—Luke 15:7

The Super Bowl telecast was the "biggie" of 1972. Over 65 million fans watched the football contest on January 16 by way of T.V. This was a new record for a sports event and broke the record of 60 million set by the last year's Super Bowl.

The game pitted brawn as well as brain before the capacity audience. What a game! What a happy ending—for some. Not all of the onlookers were satisfied with the outcome.

The game of life is also observed by a big crowd. Above us there is a great host of onlookers that watches every play of life and cheers the victories in Christ. The greatest of these victories is the eternal, everlasting, security of salvation in Christ.

Super Bowls are enjoyable, but the records are short-lived. Our Super Salvation records last for eternity.

By the way, has there been joy in heaven over your repentance and salvation?

54 A KNOW-SO INHERITANCE

"An inheritance incorruptible, and undefiled, and that fadeth not away, reserved in heaven for you."—I Peter 1:4

Frustrated estate lawyers found the clue they needed to link a woman from Edmonds, Washington, with a rural New York school teacher, Mrs. Howard, who died two years ago and left an unclaimed $100,000 inheritance.

Lawyers, checking the Howard house for valuables, discovered the yellowed letter in a shoebox containing family mementos. They located the sixty-one-year-old Mrs. Berry and informed her of her unexpected inheritance.

What a surprise and delight for Mrs. Berry! And what a tremendous inheritance! But wait a minute. I know of a better inheritance. There awaits for the Christian blessings and joys unbelievable. There is only one sad point about the inheritance awaiting the Christian. The will has been written and is waiting to be read by each of the redeemed; but, alas, days come and go without the child of God reading God's Word and rejoicing in the forthcoming inheritance.

One question my friend. How much of the "will" have you read? The inheritance came as a surprise to Mrs. Berry. Will your inheritance be as much of a surprise to you? Or do you have a "know-so" inheritance? Make it a rule of life to read a chapter a day from the "eternal will," the Word of God.

55 A WIFE'S WORTH

"She looketh well to the ways of her household, and eateth not the bread of idleness."—Proverbs 31:27

How many times a woman replies almost apologetically, "I am only a housewife." To me, however, they are unsung heroines. I became more convinced of a wife's worth after reading the following figures compiled for a financial columnist by the Chase Manhattan Bank of New York:

Job	Hours per week	Rate per hour	Total cost
Nursemaid	44.5	$2.00	$89.00
Housekeeper	17.5	3.25	56.88
Cook	13.1	3.25	42.58
Dishwasher	6.2	2.00	12.40
Laundress	5.9	2.50	14.75
Food buyer	3.3	3.50	11.55
Chauffeur	2.	3.25	6.50
Gardener	2.3	3.00	6.90
Maintenance man	1.7	3.00	5.10
Seamstress	1.3	3.25	4.22
Dietician	1.2	4.50	5.40
Practical Nurse	0.6	3.75	2.25
12 Occupations	99.6		$257.53

Ladies, my hat is off to you. Your work and your faithfulness to your work is a blessing to your husband, an example of a disciplined life to your children, and the kind of industrious dedication God expects of each of us.

A wife's worth? One thing is for sure, you can't measure a good, virtuous woman's worth in dollars and cents. Only eternity will reveal your worth and your reward, ladies.

God bless you. Good day!

56 LIBERATION TO IMMORALITY

"A woman that feareth the Lord, she shall be praised"
—Proverbs 31:30

The following articles apppeared in various newspapers:

Sept. 23, 1969—Boston (A.P.) "A coed dormitory, with men and women living on alternate floors, was approved Monday by the University of Massachusetts Board of Trustees." Two conditions had to be met. First, the 118 men in the dormitory had to approve of the venture and secondly students under twenty-one years old must have written approval of parents.

Jan. 29, 1970—Los Angeles (A.P.) "The Acacia fraternity house at the University of California at Los Angeles hasn't been the same since it got three new 'brothers'—they are girls." The article further stated, "the men dig it."

March 14, 1971—San Diego (UPI) "A men's rest room at San Diego State College was 'liberated' by coeds who said it was closer and has better lighting." The girls said they could see better to comb their hair and adjust their makeup than in a nearby women's room. An assistant dean of students said there was "nothing specific in the disciplinary rules against women using men's restrooms and vice versa."

Feb. 7, 1972—Gainesville, Fla. (AP) "About 3,000 birth control books, described as funny by some students and informative by others, have been distributed on the University of Florida Campus. The book, called *How to Take the Worry Out of Being Close,* was sponsored by the student government and all the copies were gone by the end of the first day after publication."

I have only two comments: Remember, "A woman that feareth the Lord, she shall be praised." (Prov. 31:30), and, there should be no question why Christian schools are needed today.

57 NO LONGER INCURABLE

"Jesus Christ, who is the faithful witness."—Revelation 1:5

Dr. Michael Hattwick, thirty, made medical history in November of 1970 when he, assisted by two pediatricians, saved six-year-old Matthew Winkler from dying of rabies, the terrible affliction which doctors have for thousands of years considered incurable. After this medical first, Hattwick has traveled all over the world teaching doctors the procedure.

Truly this was a tremendous effort on the part of one man to save one child. But there was a Man who expended much greater effort to save the lives of boys and girls, men and women from an even worse affliction.

Hattwick is a faithful witness to the method that was effective in saving a precious life. Christ is a faithful witness before the very throne of God that His work is effective to cure all who come to Him for salvation from sin.

It is conceivable that Hattwick's method will fail in some cases, and that the patient may die; but Christ never has, nor will He ever, lose a "patient."

Yes, there is wonderful news: sin is no longer "incurable."

58 DRIED OUT

"Ye should shew forth the praises of him who hath called you out of darkness into his marvelous light."—I Peter 2:9

The date was June 20, 1970, and I found myself engrossed in, of all things, watching a cash register repairman re-ink the register rollers. I became interested because it took him so long to do such a "simple" job. When I questioned him about it, he said, "The rollers have been dry too long and have lost some of their resiliency and pliability; therefore, the ink is absorbed very slowly."

I thought how much the rollers were like the Christian who is too long away from the Word. He becomes less pliable to God's will; he no longer "inks" a Christlike image on those with whom he comes in contact. And, invariably, the "dried out" Christian is slow to absorb the "ink" of God's dealings with him.

There is also a lesson in the time this emergency came about. The rollers went "on the blink" on Saturday afternoon—a very busy Saturday afternoon. Someone had neglected to attend to the routine servicing of the machine, and when the demand was great it could not be counted on. Isn't that the way we are caught so many times? The rush is on, the pressure is heavy, and then—*then* we realize we are "dried out."

Before the day's pressures pile on you, ask God for your daily "re-inking" so your heart will be pliable to His will all day. Don't wait until an emergency finds you all "dried out."

59 HIDDEN TREASURES

"Of Christ, in whom are hid all the treasures of wisdom and knowledge."—Colossians 2:2, 3

Alfred Stone and James Walker paid the top bid of fifty dollars for an old carved wooden trunk at an auction. They broke the lock and discovered paintings, sketches, watercolors, and engravings bearing the signature of Henry Farney, a prominent artist of yesteryear.

They were surprised and delighted to find that these paintings were valued at twenty thousand dollars, four hundred times what they had paid.

What a find! What an investment! What a profit!

Did you ever think of the investment a soul makes when one accepts Christ, the artist of all ages? His work of artistry is love, salvation, comfort, forgiveness, perfection, joy, and, as the Scripture states, "all the treasures of wisdom and knowledge."

The men had to break the lock to get to the treasures they had unwittingly bought. But with Christ each man has a key. Faith unlocks the treasures for each person. Have you found the real treasures in life in Christ? Or are they still hidden by your unbelief? Remember—*you* hold the key.

60 A REAL BARGAIN

"Evening, and morning, and at noon, will I pray, and cry aloud; and he shall hear my voice."—Psalm 55:17

A few years ago I walked down the Champs Elysees. I remember the bright colors, the bumper-to-bumper traffic—and the telephone booths where it was so difficult to make an operator understand my broken French.

A day or so ago I read about three mixed-up phones in the Champs Elysees area that allowed people to make calls all over Europe, parts of Africa, and anywhere in the United States for fifty-five centimes—one thin dime. Students, of course, were lined up outside the booths to make the "biggie call" for the "cheapie price."

Now let's analyze the situation. The price? Ten cents. The service? A long distance call. The inconvenience? A long wait in line.

In our Scripture for today David wrote that his "long distance call" went forth three times a day; evening, morning, and noon. How many times a day do we make the long distance call heavenward? The price? Not even a thin dime to us; Christ has already paid the price—His own blood. And there are no long lines, no waiting to get into the "booth." God's ear is ever ready and waiting for our call, each individual's call. And there is no time limitation. Nor is there a language problem.

I would say that was a *real* bargain, wouldn't you? The line is open—now—for you.